SOLO HARP

JOHN WILLIAMS

I. Fluffy's Harp

Witches Lullaby – Dreamily (♩ = 69-72)

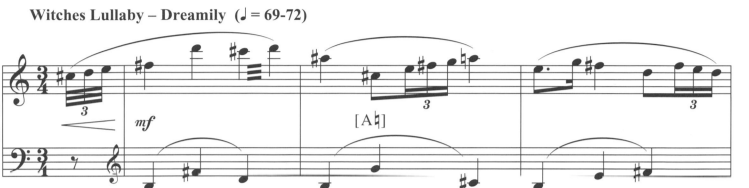

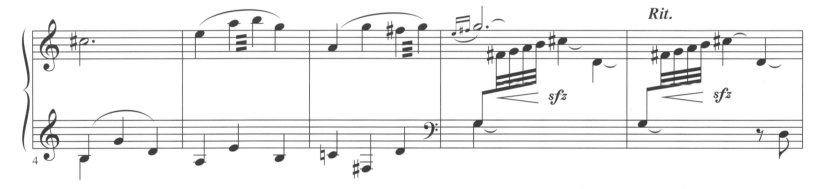

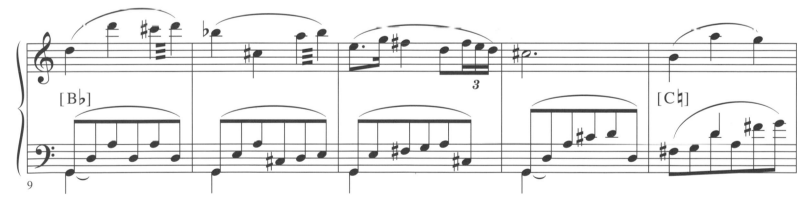

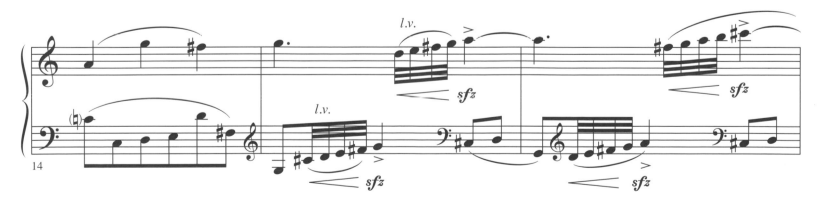

SOLO HARP

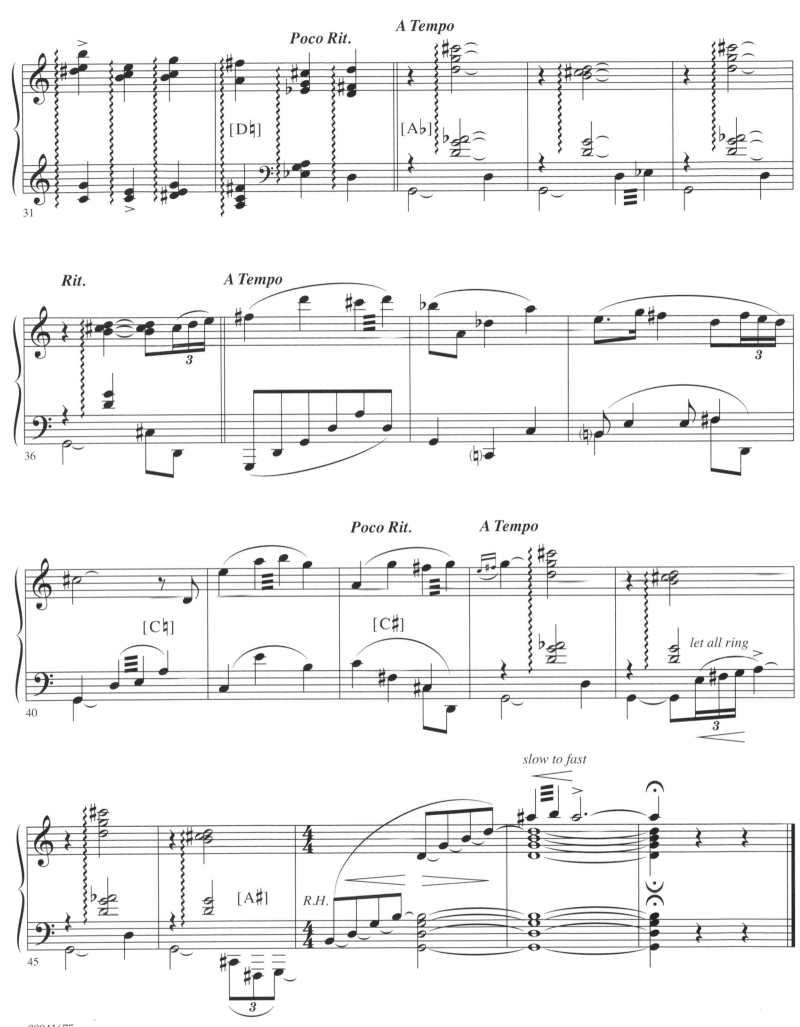

SOLO HARP

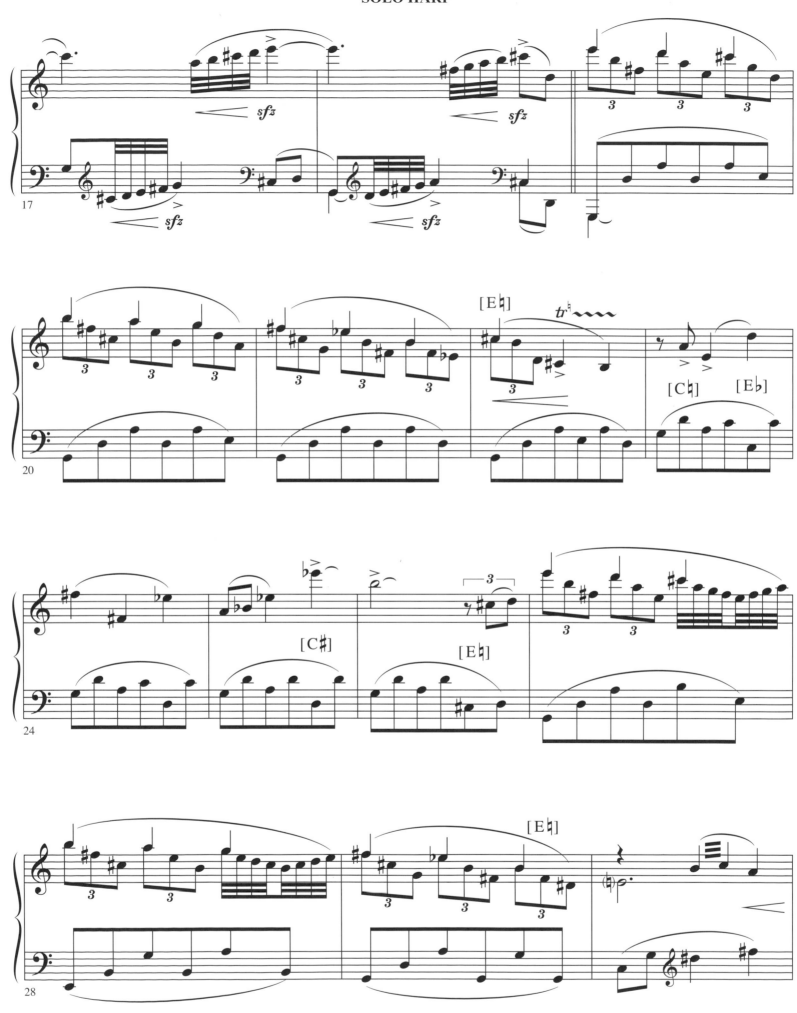

Two Themes from
HARRY POTTER
AND THE SORCERER'S STONE

SOLO HARP

JOHN WILLIAMS

II. Hedwig's Theme

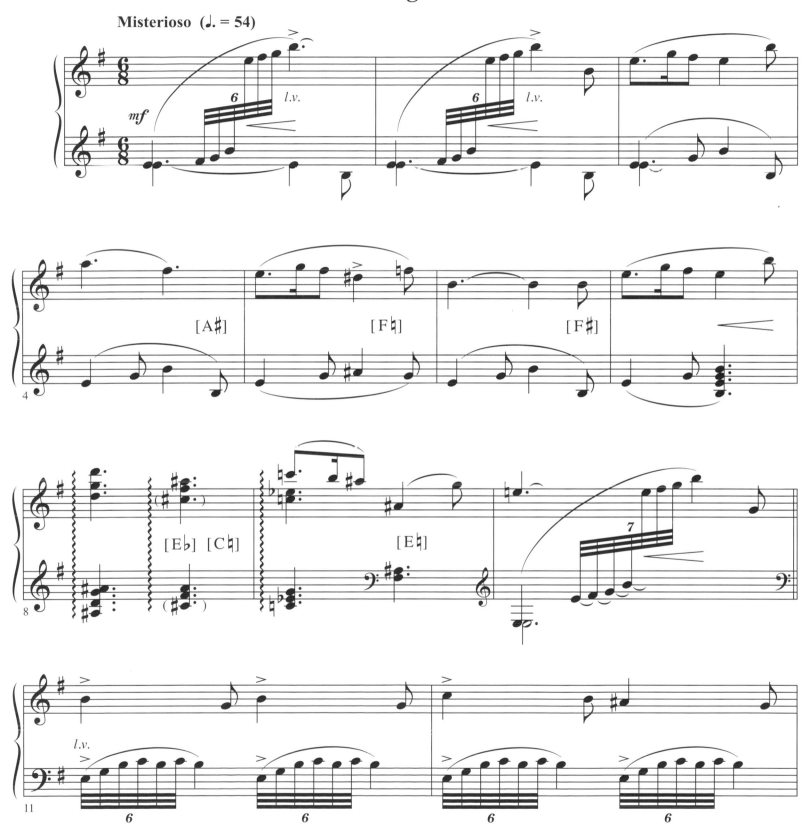

SOLO HARP

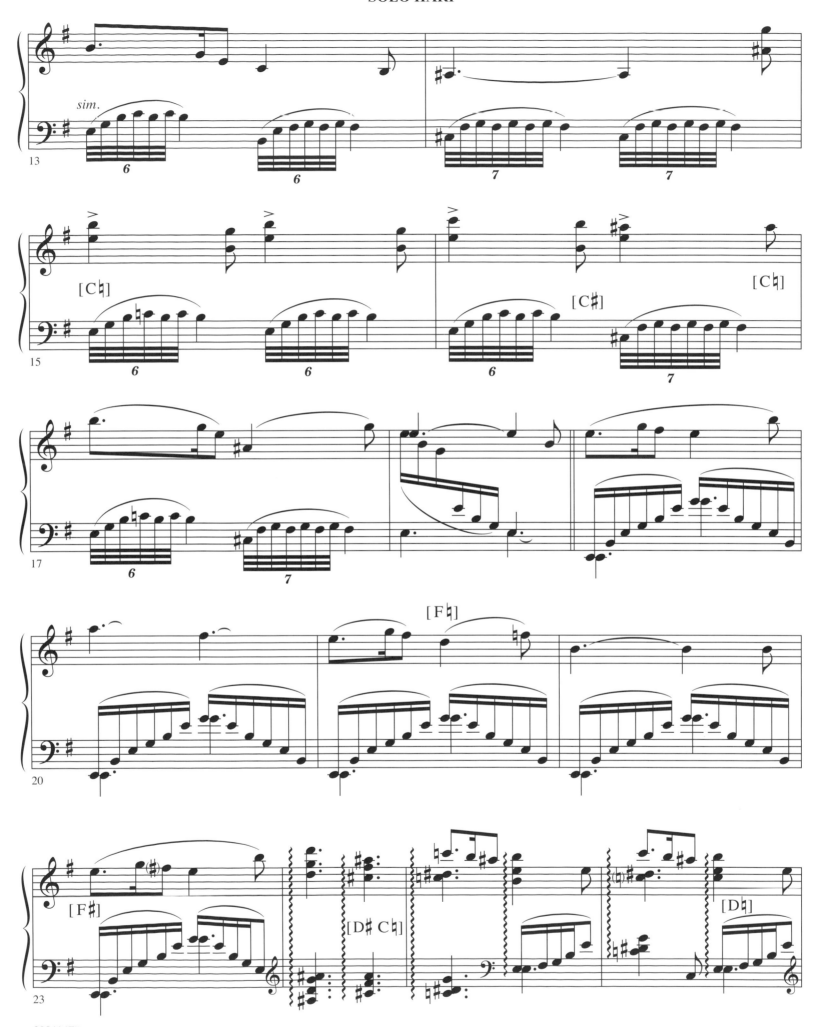